Finding Freedom In An Age of Confusion

Part 2 of The Conscious Resistance Trilogy

By Derrick Broze & John Vibes

Finding Freedom In An Age of Confusion
Table of Contents

Tools for Action

A Message From The Authors

Since releasing *The Conscious Resistance: Reflections on Anarchy and Spirituality*, we have realized the philosophy and ideas behind our perspective need to be elaborated even further. The first book in this trilogy laid the foundation for our ideas and now we want to show you the deeper levels of this way of thinking.

For many of us, being an activist, especially an anarchist one, can be a difficult road. Most of us encounter the same struggles in our path, but these struggles are rarely ever talked about. When someone "wakes up" and realizes that our society is not free, it can sometimes lead to depression, confusion, or alienation from family and friends. This is what happens when the whole world is mad and you are seeing clearly for the first time.

To help make this difficult transition easier, we decided to tackle these very personal issues and offer solutions to overcome these obstacles. In the following pages you will find essays on overcoming the depression, confusion, and fear that can come with the realization that much of the world still lives in slavery.

If book one was the body of our philosophy, consider this book the heart. We aim to show the human struggle of the search for freedom. Book 3 will examine real world application of the ideas presented in both books and could be considered the mind of our philosophy.

We have tried our best to find the beauty and positivity that surrounds us on this path and have actually found plenty of reasons to be optimistic. To be honest, both of us have also made more than a handful of mistakes and wasted much time worrying about fears that may never manifest in our everyday reality.

All of these experiences, both good and bad, have resulted in the essays contained in this book. These are our suggestions on how to navigate this crazy, beautiful world. We hope our words encourage and inspire you to continue down the path of physical, mental, and spiritual liberation.

- John Vibes & Derrick Broze, April 2016

Chapter 1 - You are a pioneer for peace

The world that we were born into and the circumstances we find ourselves in today are a vastly complicated mess of problems that have been plaguing humanity for millennia, and the idea of having a positive impact on society can leave any sane person feeling hopeless and defeated before they even get started.

The "mainstream" culture attempts to hide the harsh realities of our existence for our entire lives, so being exposed to this reality for the first time can be a deeply confusing or even traumatic process. To react with horrified aversion is a common response for many humans approached with information that contradicts the ideas around which they have built their lives. When it comes to the violence of the state and the corrupt nature of the social institutions that surround us, it is rare to see anyone absorb, reflect, and accept the information without having to rethink their worldview.

Even after discovering and seeing past the lies of the mainstream worldview, the path towards a more peaceful and free existence is incredibly difficult and frightening, and it may seem like an impossible suicide mission. This is the obstacle that prevents most people from attempting to change or criticize the society that "raised" them. If creating a free society and a world without war was easy, then you can guarantee that overnight millions of people would instantly be condemning the State and the immorality of the violence carried out by politicians and their corporate partners.

Since creating freedom where there is now slavery is a very delicate and painstaking process without an instruction manual, it may seem like a very daunting task. However, humanity is capable of incredible feats - ideas that were once seen as impossible and unthinkable are now benign and commonplace. We live in a world with tools and capabilities that would appear to be magic to our ancestors, yet we still have been unable to escape the animalistic, primitive traditions that have held humanity back for generations. We can instantly speak to people all over the world, travel to space, and store entire libraries of information on tiny thumb drives, but sadly many people still live their day to day lives in confusion and fear just as so many generations before us have.

The current era is an extremely pivotal time in the human story. We have reached that long awaited moment where humanity has become advanced enough to destroy this planet and everything on it. This massive responsibility, a responsibility that can only be met with a radical elevation in consciousness, is one which will allow our species to finally become civilized beings.

No self-respecting individual wants to look at themselves or the society that they identify with as being barbaric or uncivilized. However, when a species is killing each other by the millions, enslaving one another, and taking part in the kind of culturally justified violence that we see today, it becomes apparent that there is much work to be done before we can honestly say that humanity is "civilized".

To do what we can during our lives to leave the world and the human consciousness in better condition than when we arrived is a gravely important task but one we should not shy away from. No matter the obstacles, the goal is worth the effort. One could even argue that this is the meaning of life! It is not an easy path to take and there is no

6

guarantee that you will see the fruits of your labor in your own lifetime, but the potential of any new frontier is always shrouded in uncertainty, danger, and controversy.

The creation of the world's first free society in recorded history is simply the most recent field of exploration in the realm of human consciousness, just as space is the most recent field of exploration in the physical realm. Only one hundred years ago if you told someone you were going to build a rocket to fly people into outer space you may have run the risk of being committed to a mental hospital. Yet, despite popular opinion, the human imagination has once again defied our previous conception of reality by exploring new frontiers and pushing beyond the boundaries of what was previously thought to be possible.

If you are reading these words, then you are without a doubt in the midst of the expanding frontier that is human consciousness and thought. This is also the fight for freedom and the search for peace. You are a pioneer who has the courage to journey into uncharted territory and be your own mapmaker.

Along with millions of others worldwide who are beginning to find their purpose, you have the ability to change the world for the better in your lifetime, no matter what background you come from or where you call home. You have found yourself on a rewarding but arduous and sometimes lonely path. We know this because we have been walking this path for the better part of our lives and some years ago we passed the point of no return and we now call this path "home". Once you decide to educate yourself about the lies we are taught there is no turning back.

Chapter 2 – Reclaiming your self esteem

It is a difficult task to live in this world and remain immune to the detrimental effect which mainstream culture has on one's self esteem. Even the tyrants who themselves destroy people's self-esteem by violently imposing their will on others must live a life of mental discomfort because they are demoralized by their own actions and the world that they create.

From the moment we begin to observe the world as children, everyone around us seems so big and intimidating that we give their opinions and beliefs an undue amount of credit and sway over our decisions and opinions. In short, we give others power over us. Since our early years are so vital to our mental development and the formation of our worldview, we carry this tendency to unquestionably submit to authority throughout our entire lives.

As we grow up, various "authority" figures subject us to daily, if not hourly, judgments on our value in the community and our moral integrity. These authority figures can be found at home, at school, and in the larger society. The authorities are constantly working to undermine the self-esteem of the general population, by making these judgments and treating those in their care like second class citizens. It is not necessarily the fault of the individuals who end up in these positions of authority, as they are merely passing along the oppressive cultural norms that were forced onto them at one time or another. This does not mean that these individuals are not responsible for their actions but that they are merely a symptom of a larger problem, not the root cause.

In a world where we are constantly forced to engage with people who have complete control over us, especially from a young age, it becomes very difficult to develop any self-confidence, and the idea of living free and independent can seem absolutely horrifying to some. The rise of centralized government schooling in the past 200 years has accelerated this process by treating people like toddlers well into adulthood, causing many to develop with immature and dependent personalities.

In school we are taught how to conform to the majority, regurgitate meaningless facts, and submit to authority, but we really don't learn anything of value. That which is valuable and taught in public schools can obviously be taught and learned without government involvement, centralized control, and the overall oppressive form that these indoctrination centers have taken. It is this mechanism of control, maintained by government, which makes up the larger system responsible for the dumbing down of our society and for totally destroying an entire generation's self-esteem.

For the most crucial years of our development we are constantly getting the message that our thoughts, ideas, desires, fears, and disagreements are completely unimportant. We learn that our needs and our opinions are secondary to people in authority who are not to be questioned and who have the ability to punish or exile you at any time. This is an incredibly scary and traumatizing situation for any child, even if the repercussions are not immediately felt or seen.

These scars are then carried into adulthood, and eventually create very serious problems in the real world by causing people to act violently and irrationally, or at least make them completely miserable and obedient. Individuals who do not value themselves are often nihilistic and apathetic to changing the world for the better. Those who are lacking in personal power are also less likely to pursue radical solutions outside the accepted forms of resistance (partyarchy, voting, etc).

These are legitimate traumas that need to be recognized and worked out by everyone. The predominant culture of the Western world could easily be seen as "primitive", a place where we are subject to expectations and standards that we should not have had forced upon us. In most cases the expectations are impossible to fulfill, and in many cases are completely pointless and diametrically opposed to the individual's self-fulfillment. Realizing these simple facts is the first step in repairing one's self esteem after being beaten down by an authoritarian, soul destroying culture.

Far too many of the world's people feel inadequate and insignificant because they don't match up with the unrealistic and insane expectations that are set by the mainstream culture. Forget about those expectations and forget about those standards, they are no good for anyone and they are not a true measure of your worth. Using arbitrary traits like wealth, status, and appearance as social measurements is a recipe for disaster as it degrades human beings and sets false ideals of self-worth. It's difficult to gauge the value of someone's life by external factors, but if we must be judged, it should be according to our actions and how we treat those around us, not the superficial standards of the mainstream culture.

Chapter 3 – You are Divine

The mainstream view of history, which most state educated children are familiar with, has been handed down through the generations by the victors of past conquests. The oppressors' perspective presents the idea that great things will only be accomplished by mythical heroes who have all of the right things to say, know all of the right things to do, and who are completely devoid of fear, doubt, regret, or any other feelings of vulnerability which are part of the great spectrum of human emotion.

For the better part of history, kings and priests have created a social atmosphere in which they were these heroes, although, in reality, this ruling class was nothing like the image they put on display. In American culture the politicians are often presented in this mythical context where they are said to have the superhuman ability to know what is best for millions of other people at all times, just as the kings and priests before them. During times of social upheaval, the current ruler was naturally associated with revolutionary changes, due to the personality cult that is traditionally inherited by those in positions of power. However, this view of history relies too heavily on the individuals who have waged wars and signed declarations.

We live in a world where there are different classes of people who have different rules and different rights, according to their relationship with those in power, or their ability to use force and commit fraud upon others. Despite the predominant view that humans have equality in some form or another, the division of classes and power happens without much condemnation from the masses.

The truth is that we are equal as free, self-governing humans, but we live in societies where we are not treated as equals because small groups of sophists have established cultural norms which ensure that they are the rulers of everyone else, instead of their equals. This was obvious during the times of the monarchy and open slavery, but now the rulers hide behind democracy and communism, both ideas that claim to put the power in the hands of the people, but often end up creating the illusion of power, while strengthening the state and the ruling class.

While recognizing the limits and failures of the State's view of history, we should also remember that our current situation is only temporary and does not have to be the future of humanity. While it may be true that there are people who think they have authority over you and will probably use force to maintain that power - this does not mean that this false authority actually exists. This authority is nothing more than an illusion. The fact that the majority of the population believes in the illusion does not make this undue authority and power an objective fact. Simply put, we should not live our lives like second class "citizens" just because we are treated as such.

As beautiful, free, powerful, autonomous human beings, we can choose to be free at a moment's notice. Each and every one of us has the right to think and act as we wish, as long as we bring no harm to anyone else. In other words, you are your own king, queen, priest, authority, etc. This does not mean that we believe everyone is a "special snowflake" and should be granted certain privileges by the State in an attempt to establish equality. Rather, we believe you own yourself, regardless of how many politicians come along and claim ownership over you. You are the master of your own domain and the creator of your future. We should not live our lives as if the State is the master of our fate. Sure, we are living in a situation where our possibilities are limited and we are forced to conform in certain ways when "the powers that wish they were" are looking, but none of that changes reality, so it should not change the way we perceive our own power.

When you accept the worldview of those who oppress you and act as if it were objective truth, you are disempowering yourself and giving your abuser the upper hand. This is what happens when we attempt to conform with standards that we know are unjust, and then proceed to emotionally attack ourselves when we inevitably fall short.

It would seem our ancestors were unable to come to terms with these facts and were never able to achieve true freedom by resisting the establishment of the control systems that exist today. However, the generations born in the late 20th century and the beginning of the 21st century have tools at their disposal that their predecessors could not fathom. We have the capability and the power to turn things around and create a world where every living being has autonomy. One of the first steps towards individual and collective liberation is to claim your power, be your own master, and to make efforts to advance and spread the philosophy of self-ownership.

Chapter 4 - Trust Yourself, Vacate the State

For many free minds, learning to trust another human being can be a monumental task. The fears and doubts we pick up along our journeys might lead some to believe trust is an unworthy venture. Navigating the jungle of life can be quite difficult and learning to trust - to trust yourself, let alone another human being - may seem like a far-fetched idea, but it is essential for our development as free, conscious human beings in the pursuit of liberty.

We are pursuing liberation, not only in the physical world but of the mind, which means at some point we will also need to confront our internal tyrants. We must learn to overcome our fears and trust our own judgements and choices. We must learn to value and appreciate ourselves. From there, we can assess which individuals are worthy of certain levels of our trust. This could be anything from trusting someone to pay their share of the rent, watch your dog, build a community garden, or trusting someone with your love. Regardless of the situation, we can see value in learning to trust other human beings.

We can also see the consequences of a lack of trust within community relationships. The State not only thrives off a populace that is low in self-esteem and self-worth, but also a population that views each other with mistrust. State programs like COINTELPRO are perfect examples of the government spreading lies and disinformation in order to breed mistrust among allies. This underscores the importance of having a tight knit group of people that you can trust enough to organize community initiatives. We call this group a Freedom Cell, an idea which we will elaborate upon in book three of this series.

So, how do we avoid this? How do we avoid becoming full of doubt, mistrust and unfounded fears? Our minds can be our greatest enemies when it comes to trust. We have powerful minds and imaginations capable of dreaming up our most surreal fantasies and our worst nightmares. Many of us are still healing from deep scars created from misplaced trust. These scars can last a whole lifetime if we choose to allow it. We can exercise caution while still allowing ourselves to face the pain of being deceived or disappointed, and choose to heal from those experiences. We can choose to see ourselves for the powerful, beautiful, free human beings we are, and recognize that we deserve to be happy. We deserve to have relationships that are filled with trust, and honesty rather than fear and doubt. The State only offers a one sided relationship that does not require trust because the authorities will impose their will regardless.

In order to build empowered, self-reliant, and sustainable communities, we are going to need to trust other people in a variety of ways. Trust is essential to carving the path to a free world. As we work to trust and love ourselves and our place in this journey, we can encourage the same behavior in others. This will only make creating communities based on non-aggression, voluntary association, responsible living and empowerment, that much easier. In order to help the world continue to evolve, we need to start at home. That means starting with ourselves and our own interpersonal relationships. If the goal is an evolution of hearts and minds, it only makes sense to start with your own.

Chapter 5 - You are not alone

The process of self-discovery and learning to question the commonly accepted beliefs that most of our society holds as infallible, is not always an easy or especially fun journey. For many of us the process can be quite scary as you feel like your whole life has been turned upside down. Both of us have vivid memories of many nights spent researching the nature of government and the nature of reality itself. Sleepless nights often lead to hopeless days and depression.

When you "wake up" and challenge dogmas related to government, health, relationships, authority, and history, you may experience a journey similar to those who are grieving the loss of a loved one. In her 1969 book, *On Death and Dying*, Swiss psychiatrist Elisabeth Kübler-Ross discussed what came to be known as the Kübler-Ross model of grief. This included five different stages - denial, anger, bargaining, depression and acceptance.

This was not meant to be seen as a specific set of stages every individual will experience, or a specific order in which they may occur. Some individuals may grieve for long periods of time and experience all the stages while others may not. Still, the model offers some insight into what one may experience after challenging everything they have ever been taught or told by parents, teachers, priests, and politicians.

These feelings of anger and depression can often lead to feeling alone in a world of insanity. For far too long, people who have cared about freedom and imagined a better world for our species, have felt alone in their interests, and have been forced into the fringes of society. However, as the philosophy of freedom and non-aggression is beginning to seep into the mainstream culture, the times are changing. There has always been a portion of society who rejected authority in their hearts without ever crossing paths with another anti-authoritarian, liberation-minded individual.

Today the world is much smaller and there is now a wealth of information available to more people than ever. Our digital world allows free thinkers to cross paths with regularity, which is helping to push along the philosophical renaissance predicted in *The Conscious Resistance: Reflections on Anarchy and Spirituality*.

With that said, there is still plenty of work to be done. Unfortunately, we are fighting an uphill battle where our opponent was given a head start. The vast majority of people alive today in the Western world were molded by the state in public schools and entertained by propaganda. Many of these people have been taught a deep love and support for the status quo. Still, despite the propaganda, the human spirit is so resistant to the irrational and unnatural concept of authority that even after 12 years of indoctrination and constant manipulation, we can still overcome and free our minds.

Despite the growing awakening, you may have experienced uncomfortable situations when you try to talk about your concerns in public. This creates a situation where no one feels comfortable sharing their opinions in public and none of us truly know how many rebels exist. In reality, there are a lot more rebels out there than most people think, but many go unnoticed because human beings want to fit in, and often we will avoid speaking about uncomfortable truths or ideas to avoid being ostracized.

This is why it is important for you to start making as much noise as possible. We must let the other rebels know

17

they are not alone and encourage them to come out of hiding. Deep down we are all rebels, and the more people who step forward to admit it, the closer we will be to achieving freedom.

We are all born rebels - that is our natural state. It is only after a lifetime of being beaten down by an insane culture that we come to embrace insanity for the sake of convenience. Could it be possible that everyone out there is just pretending to go along with the status quo? It seems even those who wholeheartedly embrace it are still forced to use watered down language and euphemisms to describe the world around them because the cold hard truth is simply too much to bear.

As the State's failed policies and unsustainable practices become more obvious, the status quo will become less of a convenience for people and they will begin to open to new ideas more than ever, and the rebels will come out of hiding. These likeminded people are already all around you and the more open that you are about your own beliefs, the more open minded people you will attract.

This doesn't mean that it's a good idea to get in everyone's faces about it and create awkward situations for yourself, but it would be a wise move to begin testing the waters with subtle hints about your new found beliefs and see if anyone picks up. Find out who may be receptive to your ideas and who refuses to listen. If someone is genuinely not interested do not force your views as this will only create tension in your personal life.

It is important to remember not to be resentful and hateful towards those who cannot or will not research the information that is hiding behind the curtain. Words like "sheeple" and "statist" quickly turn from descriptors of an ignorant person, to a way to dismiss anyone who may not agree with your opinion or theory. We have to learn to accept people where they are and help those we can. The goal is collective liberation through individual empowerment, so ultimately it is up to each individual to carve their own path to freedom. Sometimes all you can do is plant seeds.

Surely, we are not the only ones who have noticed that even the "freedom movement" is quickly becoming as polarized and divided as the mainstream political circles. While it is absolutely important to remain true to your individual principles, it may not be the most productive action to immediately disregard anyone who doesn't see the world exactly as you see it.

The truth is, we all have blind spots in our thinking and we all have things to learn from other people. It is possible to have a friendly conversation with someone who sees the world completely different from you without sacrificing your beliefs, and without expecting them to sacrifice theirs.

That's not to say that there are no right or wrong answers, because in many cases there are things which can be verified and proven, but standing on opposing ends of an issue and shoving ideas down one another's throats is how the republicrats communicate. It is not how free people should communicate with each other.

For those of us standing outside of the left/right political paradigm, we see the stagnation and inefficiency that is caused by this sort of divisive approach to communication and problem solving. Debates in political circles are typically centered around attacking your opponent and showing off, instead of being focused on actually solving the problems at hand. This is one of the many reasons why the solutions to the world's problems will not come from governments as we know them today.

We must recognize that a growing number of people throughout the world are becoming disgusted with the violence and subjugation that has become commonplace in society. We all come from different backgrounds, environments, and experiences. The information that has shaped our worlds differs from individual to individual. We have entered this "movement" with different preconceived notions about why we are in this mess and how to get out.

This may seem like a dangerous and volatile situation to someone used to seeing people with different opinions tear each other apart, but in reality this is a beautiful gift that we should all embrace as we attempt to learn from each other. If we think of the global situation as a giant puzzle, we can describe all of these different people with different viewpoints as a unique piece in that puzzle that is essential for its completion.

Some of us may be conservative on certain issues and liberal on others. We may call ourselves voluntaryists or libertarians, constitutionalists or Anarchists. We may be socialists or futurists, communists or individualists. We may disagree on a range of ideas, but the bottom line is that we have a great deal to learn from one another.

There is no way we are going to fight the mercantilist monster that stands before us if we don't respect one another's opinions and banish the idea that someone with a different opinion may actually have something valid to teach.

As free thinkers we should celebrate the moment that we learn new information, even if that information may cause us to change our minds and feel differently about certain things. *ESPECIALLY* if that information causes us to change our minds. The ability to overcome one's own ego and humbly change your mind when presented with new information is one of the fundamental characteristics of a "free thinker".

Again, we want to be clear that this does not mean that you should go around agreeing with what everyone says, or that you can't be firm in your convictions, but it is just as important to remember that we are in this fight to solve problems and reduce the level of accepted violence. We are not here to break each other down and further divide our world. We are here to teach, learn, and build a better world.

Engaging in debates with people who are deeply entrenched in their own worldview may have some importance and value, but you will be disappointed if you expect to find likeminded people through this process. That's not to say you shouldn't associate or discuss philosophy with people who disagree with you, because you absolutely should; but the more often we interact and connect with our brothers and sisters of similar worldview and goals, the more we contribute to a paradigm shift of hearts and minds.

A paradigm shift is a process in which individuals gain new knowledge which completely alters and evolves their understanding of the world. We believe we are currently experiencing a paradigm shift that has been taking place for generations with increasing awareness in the last decades of the 20th century. By educating yourself about the hidden truths of the world and seeking solutions that empower each of us, you are contributing to this paradigm shift.

As the State continues its death march and eventual collapse, it will become increasingly important to build communities in the digital and physical worlds. Together, we can educate each other and create solutions which put an end to systematic oppression, and allow the human spirit to flourish.

Chapter 6 – Learn from everyone, but be your own teacher

It is important to exercise your ability to learn from every person and situation that we experience. Never allow yourself to limit your knowledge by ignoring information that may be contrary to your viewpoints. Even after reading our work, we urge each of you to continue your research so you can form your own unique opinions about what's going on in the world. No single source of information should be the foundation of your world view. This dependency is equivalent to giving another person the power of thinking for you.

Much of the western world has been taught to look at society in a very polarized way. When certain issues are presented to us through mainstream circles, they are typically oversimplified to the point where all concepts are presented as black or white - as if there are always clear "good guys" and "bad guys".

The reality of the situation is that life is often more complicated than that. There are usually many different ways of looking at things and many different sides to every story. This is especially true in the study of philosophy where terms are constantly being redefined and ideas constantly reexamined with every new generation of philosophers.

When it comes to the idea of governance, the situation is more complex than simply picking a political party or social clique and subscribing yourself to a whole system of beliefs based on other people's ideas. Unfortunately, this is the kind of approach that is generally embraced worldwide, partly because this is how we have been taught to think. Also. because it's a lot easier than doing all of the rigorous research and contemplation necessary to get to the bottom of important social issues.

Especially today, with the incredible amount of contradictory information that is available on the internet, people are becoming increasingly overwhelmed when trying to separate fact from fiction. Sifting through all of this information and cross-referencing sources is time consuming and not easy for some, but it's a necessary part of achieving any kind of certainty in your research.

This is the difference between coming to your own conclusions rather than adopting the conclusions of others. There are plenty of people out there with great ideas, and there's nothing wrong with having trusted researchers that you regularly look to for reliable information, but don't take anyone's word at face value and don't disregard information purely on the source, without confirming its inaccuracy for yourself.

There are plenty of researchers out there who are very knowledgeable and on point in some respects, while still uninformed and off base in many other areas on which they comment. This is why we should critically assess all of the information we come across, and search for alternative views to get a well-rounded idea of what we are trying to figure out. There are researchers out there who are brilliant in terms of analyzing foreign policy, but who have terribly misguided views on economics, and vice versa.

No one is perfect and we should all be aware of our own strong and weak positions so we may continue to learn and grow. This is exactly why it is important to look up everything for ourselves, and check the source documentation to confirm that the information we are receiving is accurate. No one has all the right answers all the time, and if someone pretends to, you might want to proceed with extra caution.

For far too long, learning has been a top down process in our culture. It is up to each of us to educate ourselves and our communities using the power of the internet and other cutting edge tools, so that we may continue to mine one of the most vital resources on the planet - the human imagination.

Chapter 7 - Understanding family and friends

As we move from examining our internal relationships to the world at large, we want to take a moment to discuss the difficulties that often come from explaining your newfound views and opinions to your closest family and friends. One of the main things preventing us from actually achieving peace and freedom, is the simple fact that many people who actually are unhappy with the status quo are too afraid to speak out, because they are worried about what their parents, friends, or even complete strangers will think of them.

Whether you believe the world is being corrupted by a cabal of government officials, banking institutions, military interests, reptilian aliens, or some mix, we generally understand that there are rebellious minds out there that question official proclamations made by government agents, police officers, and media pundits. Whether we come to the same conclusions or solutions does not yet matter. We appreciate all those who choose to peek behind the veil of Statism and authority. Personally, we both believe the State, as an institution, is immoral, and the majority of the world's government are corrupt pawns for various interests that operate in the shadows.

Maybe your view is not as extreme, but chances are if you are reading this book, your views could be classified as outside the "mainstream". There's also a good chance you have spent some nights researching on the internet, watching documentaries, and rearranging your worldview. You have likely attempted to share this information via social networks, internet forums, and casual conversations with friends and family. Perhaps you are now comfortable proclaiming to your loved ones that you have "woken up" and have begun chastising them for not taking action and joining the revolution! Unless you're one of the lucky ones, you were, unfortunately, probably met with silence or straight up mockery.

This silence and rejection may lead to feelings of anger and resentment that can cause real damage to important relationships. For those of us who feel like we have discovered long hidden truths, it can be extremely disheartening to have our close friends and family turn a blind eye, with our words falling on deaf ears. Remember, sometimes your job is only to plant seeds, not to constantly attempt to "convert" people to your perspective.

We understand that tumbling down certain rabbit holes can lead to life-altering revelations - new values, new principles, and a new understanding of the world - which leads to a reassessment of the types of relationships you keep. Some individuals will choose to disown family members and friends over differences that are deemed to be too great to continue the relationship. While we do not believe free individuals should be obligated to maintain *any* relationship which is counter-productive or destructive (whether blood relative or not), we also think this decision should not be taken lightly.

Simply appreciating an individual for where they are on their path can also be of value. We are all at different points in our journeys. This does not mean you should abandon your values, but remember that everyone is learning. Have compassion for those who do not see what you have come to see. Lead by example and others will be encouraged to begin their own search for answers.

Chapter 8 - The state is not invincible, it's just a bad idea

Throughout humanity's history, war after war has been waged against various forms of authority, only to lead to further subjugation. This happens because the people are often mesmerized by yet another "savior" promising hope and change, while truly chasing after "power". To understand this drive for power and control we must understand power itself.

The traditional definition of power is "the ability to control people or things" or "political control of a country or area". Power, like any tool, can be used to create positive or negative outcomes depending on one's perspective. There are also different types of power. There is power over another person and there is also power that is diffused or shared among a group of people. Political power could be seen as the exercise of constraint on people's action.

On Thanksgiving Day 1980, radical American Indian activist and poet John Trudell spoke about the illusion of power:

"We have to re-establish our identity. We have to understand who we are and where we fit in the natural order of the world, because our oppressor deals in illusions. They tell us that it is power, but it is not power. They may have all the guns, and they may have all the racist laws and judges, and they may control all the money, but that is not power. These are only imitations of power, and they are only power because in our minds we allow it to be power. But it's all an imitation. Racism and violence, racism and guns, economics- the brutality of the American Corporate State way of life is nothing more than violence and oppression and it doesn't have anything to do with

power. It is brutality. It's a lack of a sane balance. The people who have created this system, and who perpetuate this system, they are out of balance. They have made us out of balance. They have come into our minds and they have come into our hearts and they've programmed us. Because we live in this society, and it has put us out of balance. And because we are out of balance we no longer have the power to deal with them. They have conquered us as a natural power.

We are power. They deal in violence and repression, we are power. We are a part of the natural world. All of the things in the natural world are a natural part of the creation and feed off the energy of our sacred mother, Earth. We are power. But they have separated us from our spiritual connection to the Earth, so people feel powerless. We look at the oppressor and we look at the enemy because they have the most guns and the most lies and the most money. People start to feel powerless... They want us to believe that we are powerless.

We are a natural part of the earth, we are an extension of that natural energy. The natural energy which is Spirit, and which is power. Power. A blizzard is power. An earthquake is power. A tornado is power. These are all things of power that no oppressor, no machine age, can put these things of power in a prison. No machine age can make these things of power submit to the machine age. That is natural power. And just as it takes millions and billions of elements to make a blizzard to happen, or to make the earthquake, to make the earth to move, then it's going to take millions and billions of us.

We are power. We have that power. We have the potential for that power."

As Trudell points out, power is more than just the physical mechanisms of the State, more than politicians who can be voted out or even imprisoned. There have been countless battles to overthrow the established powers, but none of them have resulted in freedom for humanity in the long term. This is because all of these struggles were being fought on the wrong battlefield. Obviously, dealing with the physical manifestations of oppression will be a part of any evolutionary movement, but we must recognize the fight that exists beyond the physical realm. That is, the internal struggle between your desire for freedom, and your internal tyrants desire to bend your will to authority.

The oppressed have always thought we were fighting against people, when we are truly engaged in a war of ideas. Without a doubt, slavery and physical abuse exist and have resulted in a great deal of damage and destruction. But let's imagine that all the slave masters, policy makers, and bureaucrats who approved of "legal" slavery and abuses, were suddenly removed from the equation. Would that end slavery and the inherent injustices of the State? No. The ideas and the widespread acceptance of such ideas which allowed them to commit their crimes without consequence, would still remain. This leaves the door open for future authoritarians to repeat the process. As long as someone holds a desire to wield organized power for their own means (whether benevolent or not), there is a risk of the State being recreated and inevitably growing beyond the control of the people.

Yet when we look around at our world today, it is obvious this concept is still not understood by the majority of the population, who have the understandable, but misguided tendency to think that violence is going to solve their problems. For far too long, our species has used violence as a tool to achieve our goals. Violence has been at the very basis of social organization and problem solving for the better part of history. This may be why some people are so quick to resort to violence in any conflict - they have learned it from the State!

Perhaps, we have become desensitized to the use of violence after a lifetime of witnessing government and their mercantilist corporate partners employ violence in the form of war, taxation, ecological destruction, and outright slavery. We must unlearn the narrative that has been provided and rewrite our understanding of the nature of government and human relations in general.

One of Albert Einstein's most famous quotes is: "Problems cannot be solved by the same level of thinking that created them." This applies perfectly to the situation we are discussing, and sheds light onto why the violent revolutions of the past were never able to achieve their goal of setting the human race free from authority.

Since birth, the establishment has fed us perpetual lies and, unfortunately, even when someone discovers the violent nature of that establishment, they are still met with the task of sifting through everything they have ever been told to see what was true and what was not. When that backtracking doesn't take place, it is common for people to get caught up in the vengeful mentality that comes along with learning about one's own enslavement. When lies about "human nature" or the capabilities of our species are still not recognized and addressed, then it is very hard for people to wrap their minds around nonviolent and apolitical solutions to the problems we see in the world today.

The State and all of its predatory appendage, like the corporate and military industrial complexes, are not simply groups of people with weapons who need to be overthrown; they are just bad ideas that can very easily be rendered obsolete with the right combination of good ideas. The first battlefield that the revolution needs to be won on, is the mind. To destroy the problems that were created with violence, the most effective weapons are good ideas and nonviolent solutions - not continued violence and failed politics.

Chapter 9 – The golden age is tomorrow, not yesterday

Every generation that has walked the earth was unable to imagine or comprehend what tomorrow would bring. This inability to anticipate coming changes causes many to believe their moment in history, and what they see in their day to day life, is humanity's maximum level of advancement and understanding of the world. Generation after generation has been proven wrong as we continue to advance in both our understanding of the world and our ability to impact society at large. Even still, there are many who live their lives as if humanity has stopped evolving.

Those living with this mentality often espouse an intense nostalgia for an era they themselves were not around to see, but which has been idealized by older generations in the stories that have been handed down through the ages. When politicians and leaders make mistakes and things go wrong, as they often do, the population does not know where to look for inspiration, and instead dwells on the image of the "good ol days", which has been imprinted in their mind since childhood. If only the people were to look for inspiration within their own hearts, minds, and communities, the ruling class would surely tremble in their ivory towers.

While every nation and people may have their own Golden Age myth, in America, children are indoctrinated with a love of the founding fathers and the myth of limited constitutional government. It is a deeply ingrained idea that, while things may be a bit screwed up now, once upon a time there were these heroic and selfless aristocrats called the founding fathers who birthed a nation, helping make the people free and prosperous. We are also told that generally everyone loved them and was happy. This is the cartoonish version of events that plays out in our history books and the cultural myths that are so present in our everyday lives. However, this nationalistic folklore has nothing to do with reality and completely ignores the history of oppression and violence unleashed on the thousands of tribes and nations who were already living in what came to be known as the United States of America.

America's founding fathers may have expressed brilliant ideas and helped spread the general idea of freedom, they are not perfect. There are some core philosophical principles they did a great job enshrining (at least in theory; in reality these principles only applied to rich, white men) for future generations to carry on. However, many of these people were still quite oppressive both in their personal and political lives. Many of these men owned slaves, and were racist, classist, and sexist. They were also not as popular in their own times as the history books describe either. The politicians of the past, even in early America were just as unpopular as politicians of our time and the founding fathers were no different.

There were constant rebellions among the general population in the generation surrounding the Declaration of Independence, because people rightly saw their local colonial government just as oppressive as the British Empire. These rebellions were often met with brutal force by the aristocrats who are idealized in American history books as the nation's founding fathers. Nevertheless, people took up arms and risked their lives fighting against the government, as we saw in Shay's Rebellion and the Whiskey Rebellion, against George Washington.

In some ways, people living during this time were probably significantly more free than your average person today, as they had to deal with fairly little government intervention in comparison to us. However, this was still a rough time and place to live because the political structure was responsible for an extremely low standard of living among the general population. With that being the case, it's pretty safe to say that America's founding should not be looked at as a golden age worthy of repetition.

Humanity's history has been one of constant but slow progression towards a more free society. Slowly but surely, one by one, generation by generation, we shed the insane and irrational political ideas that previously held our ancestors captive. When approached from this angle, it may seem counterproductive to reach into the past to find a path toward a free society. There are plenty of lessons that can be learned from studying history, yet we should seek to combine the best of yesterday with the ever-evolving present reality and accumulated knowledge. In our previous book, we discuss the land known as Zomia as an example of a past society we could learn from, and we would also suggest a reading of Pierre Clastres' *Society Against the State* for those interested in further reading on past societies with radical ideas about self-organization and government.

One of the great mysteries of the world, is the repetitious cycle of history and how our species continues to make the same mistakes over and over again. This cycle probably has many different causes, but the cultural myth of the golden age is without a doubt a contributor. Thousands of years ago, republics and democracies were seen as the ideal ways to organize society, but time and experience have shown that these systems of government breed corruption just like any system of coercive social control inevitably does. This corruption resulted in an economic and cultural collapse that was spread out across the whole civilized world and lasted many generations.

With the democratic and republican systems of government a proven failure, our ancestors had an opportunity to create a free society in its ashes. Unfortunately, this did not happen. This is due, in part, to the fact that the minds of the masses were still trapped in the paradigm of domination. So while they may have escaped their physical chains, they failed to overcome these ideas on a philosophical level.

Putting an end to tyranny isn't accomplished by simply overthrowing a tyrant. There is no treaty that can be signed to prevent other tyrants from rising in their place. The prevalence of violence and oppression on a mass scale is only able to continue as long as the general population is conned into believing the status quo is the best possible outcome. The powers that wish they were would like you to believe that their money, military, media, and "authority" has achieved as close to a utopia as humanity can come.

However, when the masses decide the violence of the ruling class is immoral and socially unacceptable, it will be impossible for tyrants to convince anyone to take part in their madness. This is what is meant by "philosophically overcoming" violent ideas, rather than changing the person sitting on the throne or signing documents.

At the fall of the Roman Empire the paradigm was not changed, there was no philosophical advancement. In fact, there was actually a regression to long term feudalism. Perhaps this came as a result of the collective fear of pursuing the unknown (freedom) and the comfort of the past (slavery). This is just one prominent example that relates to today's political climate, but history is rife with examples of people making the same mistakes over and over again by embracing the same bad ideas of the previous regime.

Today we find ourselves in another time of great change. From our perspective, the established powers are on shaky ground and the general population is starting to realize the way of life that has been hoisted upon them is unsustainable and a new path is necessary. This happens regularly every few generations, but unfortunately, every single time there has been a revolution or social upheaval, the worldview has remained the same and the cycle was not broken.

The pain, depression and confusion that can come from admitting the twisted nature of our day to day existence, seems to be too much for most people to cope with. That being the case, they create extremely complex justifications and rationalizations for the violence and insanity taking place around them. This is how our species has gotten to where it is today, with numerous brutal empires stretching across the entire globe, to the point where there is no longer the option to escape to the promised land. With the general population in a constant state of denial for many generations, the people and organizations that controlled the world's land and resources have been able to consolidate their power with minimal resistance. This is a process that has been taking place since the dawn of civilization.

People often mistakenly believe the revolution started right at the moment when they became aware of it. In reality, the battle between freedom and enslavement has been raging for centuries, and has played out like a relay race where each generation passes the mission along to the next. The only problem is that those on the side of freedom have not had the ability to participate in this process. For the better part of history, the general population was illiterate and poorly educated, making it that much more difficult to immortalize their side of the story and their ideas for future generations.

Meanwhile, those who sought to enslave humanity were very familiar with planning beyond their own time, as it often took many generations to complete large projects, such as palaces, bridges and monuments. Military conquests were known to take several generations as well. The ruling class has grown accustomed to long term plans and goals that outlasted their own lifetimes. With most of humanity simply surviving (as opposed to thriving) for the better part of history, it has been hard for people to see past their next meal, so the idea of planning for future lifetimes was probably not very common. However, we do see an example of thinking of future generations in the *Constitution of the Iroquois Nations*. The Constitution of the Iroquois Nation has helped popularize this idea, often known as the principle of seven generations, or simply considering the impact of your actions on the unborn. The Constitution reads:

Cast not over your shoulder behind you the warnings of the nephews and nieces should they chide you for any error or wrong you may do, but return to the way of the Great Law which is just and right. Look and listen for the welfare of the whole people and have always in view not only the present but also the coming generations, even those whose faces are yet beneath the surface of the ground – the unborn of the future Nation.

Under the current paradigm of sophisticated mental conditioning via the media and government schools, people have been trained to live as if they were the last generation on earth. Many people continue to pass along the mentality of their oppressors onto their children as their ancestors did to them. Luckily, thanks to the widespread decentralization of information that has been made possible by the internet, there are now more people than ever who are starting to question the nature of society and political power.

This is a great victory in the struggle for freedom, but unfortunately many people become depressed and discouraged when coming to the reality of their existence. A world of peace and rationality seems like such a total stretch of the imagination, because it is drastically different from what we experience today - but this does not mean a better world is impossible.

With each and every generation, there are many drastic paradigm shifts that radically alter the way the people interact with each other. Taking a long view of history, it could be said that these shifts are contributing to a slow upward progression towards a more peaceful world. Unfortunately, tragedies like mass murder, slavery, and subjugation still take place, but they are getting harder and harder to justify because our species is in the process of evolving beyond the type of mentalities that trigger such behavior.

When approached from this perspective, it becomes obvious that freedom and peace are inevitable for our species. This does not mean that you should just sit back and wait for it to happen. No, we need you to be actively engaged, using your intellect and energy towards outgrowing the violent social systems that we were all born into. Together we can make the shift happen sooner rather than later.

By noting that the revolution will be won over many generations, we are not claiming the current generation can not make great progress and lay a solid foundation for a free society. We are simply stating that although it may seem like this moment in time is the climax of the human story, every person who is alive right now was born into an age old revolution that will eventually be carried on by future generations. We all have the potential to discover, develop, and share new ideas which will help lay the foundation for the first truly free society that has ever existed.

Chapter 10 - Building a more free, connected and compassionate world

The idea of the State is forced onto each of our lives from the moment we are born. We are told there is only one way of life, one path towards freedom and happiness. On that path is the idea that the government (and taxes) are inevitable. This path is backed up by the belief that the current forms of the State we see around the world, are the pinnacle of our evolution. We don't believe this to be true. We are at a point where humans can connect, communicate, interact with, and learn from people all around the world. Ideas are spread with a speed never before seen. A concept can evolve very quickly, with input and criticism from many places all at once. Just as ideas for better technology and more efficient methods to live our lives are developing, so is our understanding of freedom.

We are growing to respect each other's individual freedom and choosing to take responsibility for our own lives and doing what we can to help others in our community. As we learn to value freedom and respect towards all life on this planet, we are also choosing to focus inward, to look within ourselves for answers about what it means to be a part of a global community in a world that marches towards unsustainable living. As every individual that makes up the global community chooses self-reflection and begins to understand humanity's place in the bigger picture, we will also develop a deeper understanding of liberty and come to reject the parental trappings of government we have become accustomed to.

As each of us decide to reflect on our paths in this experience, we awake to the beautiful dangerous freedom that is sovereign living. We begin to recognize that the idea of government as a parent figure is silly and that we don't

41

need our hands held anymore. As minds begin to wake from the matrix, the effects will create shock waves that ripple through our very existence. We will realize that our attempts to wage war to bring peace have failed. For possibly the first time in our history, mankind will release the pain, the fear that we have been holding onto, and we will step forth into the light to claim our role as warriors for peace, both teacher and student.

At this point, we believe, at least some portion of humanity will choose self-governance and voluntarily engage in community representation, or government. Communities that are built on the ideas of compassion, sovereignty of the individual, mutual aid, and sustainable practices. *The Conscious Resistance* is predicated on the belief that individuals who know themselves best are more suited for the physical, intellectual, and spiritual pursuit of liberation. But empowered minds will only succeed when we choose to voluntarily organize and create the conscious Agoras of the future. This, of course, is going to take some work. The good thing is that it starts with each of us on the individual level. By choosing to take action, and make change in your life today, in this moment, you are contributing to the evolution of hearts and minds.

Chapter 11 - The sky may be falling, but it's only a storm

As more people become aware that something just isn't quite right in the world, the police state has gone into overdrive to counteract this growing resistance to the status quo. We will be the first to admit, that the growing police and surveillance states are only a piece of the many serious issues that must be faced by our species. However, we also see many reasons to feel optimistic about the future of humanity.

The more aware the populace becomes, the more frantic the media, government, and corporate partners become. Their whole scam is dependent upon their control over the human consciousness, and that control is beginning to unravel. This is the equivalent to someone in a debate screaming ad hominem attacks when faced with an argument superior to their own.

When a thief or liar is exposed you often see them act out in verbal or even physical aggression. It is not unusual for guilty parties to act outraged about accusations against them and then to paint the victim as a villain. This is exactly what has been playing out in the macrocosm of geopolitics, as more and more people are becoming aware of their enslavement. As the leaders and authorities are exposed as illegitimate, the establishment is lashing out with all their might.

History is full of societies and empires collapsing and rebuilding. If the people of today are willing to work together and cooperatively face adversity, they may be able to weather any potential storm and emerge stronger than before. There is no doubt that we are in the midst of a storm that has been raging for centuries, and the intensity of that storm is growing by the minute. We have every reason to make any and all preparations that we deem to be necessary, but we should not be consumed by fear to the point where we are considering violence or nihilism. The reason why there is so much fear surrounding the downfall of the state is because people have grown detached from their communities and have lost their ability to be self-sufficient.

With that being the case, the first step towards overcoming that fear and preparing for the oncoming storm is to get more familiar with your community and start thinking about ways in which you can expand your skills and knowledge. Growing food, getting to know your neighbors, establishing community study groups, and learning about off the grid solutions are just a few ways to strengthen your family and your community, as living standards continue to deteriorate. (In our next book we plan to elaborate on ideas for building off the grid community solutions.)

There seems to be a fascination with talking about "the end of America" or the end of the world. Some people believe everyone alive today would somehow forget all we have learned as a species and return to pre-industrial living conditions simply because the government and their fiat currency failed. This is completely false and ignores the ingenuity of the human mind. While we are still dealing with the dictatorship of the State, we must remain vigilant and not become overwhelmed with what they throw at us, this is exactly what they are trying to provoke.

The establishment wants us paralyzed with fear so they can prevent us from making any moves that might rock the boat. We cannot row the boat to safety without rocking it, so we must find the courage within ourselves to make waves instead of sitting around waiting for the boat to row itself or waiting for the deranged captain to rescue us.

We can and must recognize the injustices taking place in our world today. We can and must identify the mechanisms and people behind these injustices. We must not be scared into thinking that the status quo is our only option, or that we are fighting a losing battle. Defeatist attitudes will prevent us from making any real progress. While we should remain aware of the dangers posed by the oppressors, we should not fear them. If we combine education with action and work to dismantle the lies, violence, and fear we can regain control of our own lives and liberate ourselves from this Matrix.

Chapter 12 – The illusion of race

Every human being is a unique individual. We each have different thoughts, different inspirations, different hair, eye and skin color. These differences should all be embraced as it shows that everyone is bringing a unique and enlightening perspective to the table for humanity. Sadly, those who seek to control us use these differences to put us against each other, and take the heat off of themselves.

Throughout the history of imperialism our "rulers" have conditioned us to be frightened and hostile towards those who are not under their rule. That is because our rulers either wish to enslave these other people, or take their land and resources, or both.

In order to carry out war and conquest it was necessary for rulers to infect their subjects with blind nationalistic ideologies. People were trained from birth to think of their nationality as being superior to all others. Citizens were taught that people who lie outside the domain of their ruler were sub human, their lives were said to be less valuable than those that were inside of the kingdom.

Imposing this kind of twisted world view made it possible for kings and emperors to use their citizens as mercenaries and gate keepers. This is how racism was invented, as a mental justification for conquest and the brutality of the ruling class.

By using fear tactics and generalizations, those in power have managed to turn everyone in the world against one another so they can play war games amongst themselves, using us as the pieces.

Some of the darkest moments in human history were the result of mob frenzies fueled by racist ideologies. The crusades, the German holocaust, the Native American holocaust, the African holocaust, and various forms of slavery have all been carried out under the racist visions of various ruling class psychopaths. Each time it has been a different control freak, from a different corner of the earth, with the same list of excuses and a similar set of dehumanizing epitaphs.

This is happening in any country with an imperialistic, dominating system of government, just as it has for centuries. Although the mass majority of people are more conscious now and are opposed to racism, the elite still project a very racist message through the media and through their social policies. This influence has a very serious impact on the acceptance of the current occupation in the Middle East and the corporate rape and pillaging of the 3rd world.

Humanity as a whole wants to move past this barbaric self-destruction but the aristocracy and their dominant political systems create a social environment where certain groups are at a disadvantage due to their ethnicity.

The establishment is constantly promoting racism and creating social injustice under the radar, regardless of what they say in the public arena. This has been the policy of the ruling class for centuries and is still very much alive today just in a more subtle subliminal form.

Unfortunately, racism is alive and well today in the form of ethnocentrism and nationalism. Both of these words mean the same thing, but ethnocentrism would be a more realistic description that carries a more negative stigma.

The Merriam Webster Dictionary defines ethnocentrism as *"the belief in the inherent superiority of one's own ethnic group or culture"* and defines Nationalism as *"loyalty and devotion to a nation; especially : a sense of national consciousness exalting one nation above all others and placing primary emphasis on promotion of its culture and interests as opposed to those of other nations or supranational groups"*.

Both of these definitions describe a dressed up form of racism. These ideologies are an attempt to justify or rationalize aggression against another group of people. These are cultural assumptions which are rooted in falsities and continue due to a lack of understanding.

Regardless of the color of our skin, the language we speak or the cultural ideologies we subscribe to, we are all a part of the same human family. In every country throughout the ages we have been deceived by our oppressors. People of all nationalities struggle and suffer at the hands of conniving sophists, who tell us that other oppressed people in some far away land are the reason for our unhappiness.

In reality, the oppressed people of all nations have more in common with each other than they do with the people in charge of their governments. Unfortunately, we have all been lied to and conditioned to be suspicious of our brothers and sisters. Our real enemies are the snakes that promote subversive racist political systems and put the human organism on a path of self-destruction.

Chapter 13 – Another look at the doomsday myth

With the constant barrage of news headlines and media pundits warning of the impending doom of our civilization, many people have begun to prepare for the possibility of a period with fewer modern conveniences than we have today. Some would call these people careful, others would call them prudent or wise, some might even call them paranoid, but these days the mainstream media has branded these people as "Doomsday Preppers". This title not only works to discredit people who seek to be independent and get off the grid, but also perpetuates the myth that doomsday is even coming.

It is true that *something* is coming, the signs are all around us - a deteriorating economy, rampant global war, and an overall unsustainable system of governance. So if it's not doomsday, then what is everyone preparing for, and where is all this madness leading us? If doomsday means the possible downfall of "civilization" perhaps we need to start viewing this event in a new light. The end of the status quo could be the greatest thing to ever happen to humanity. This could be the final fall of "Babylon".

Think of it this way: millions of people feel helpless because they see the madness in our world and search for the root causes, but cannot conceive of a way to make change that does not include working within the current system. Meanwhile, this system is overthrowing itself right in front of us. Many of us wish that the government could be overthrown, yet we fear it's inevitable collapse when we should be embracing it. If the U.S. government (and other western nations) continues on their current path, a significant reduction in quality of life and geopolitical influence is inevitable.

In the United States, the Federal Reserve System props up the economy with more debt and fake money. Without the Fed performing this act of economic magic, the average American would likely be more aware of the theft and loss of value taking place right in front of their eyes. The Ruling Class would have no method for hiding the miserable state of affairs, and the masses would be spurred to action. Either way, the charade is going to end eventually. They can only play this game for so long before hyperinflation takes effect and topples their already fragile house of cards.

This presents an incredible opportunity for the human race. If we are adequately prepared in terms of getting our physical needs met, as well as developing the mental and philosophical maturity that is required for the establishment of a free society, we can create a network of autonomous, individually sovereign communities. While the world seems to be descending into insanity all around us, it is important for us as individuals to assess the kinds of goods and services that may be needed after an economic collapse and devise peaceful, sustainable methods by which we can provide these values to our families and communities. (In our next book we plan to elaborate on ideas for building off the grid community solutions.)

The Ruling Class and the complex of military, biotechnology, banking, media, and corporate entities are not blindly pushing towards destruction without a plan in mind. When the opportunity presents itself, this cabal will seek to create order out of chaos and implement their own sadistic plans for the human race. However, they will only be able to create their authoritarian slave farm if the slaves themselves ask for this and assist in creating it. The slaves (the general population to varying degrees) will only ask for this deeper enslavement if they are unaware of its consequences and see no possible alternatives.

This is why it is important for each us to develop solutions to meet our needs - and the needs of our neighbors, without depending on the initiation of the use of force, as that is a method of doing business which has destroyed civilizations time and time again. Likewise, it is equally important for us to advance a proper understanding of philosophy and of our current situation, so the population is socially mature enough to be their own masters, and to accept the new and unusual nonviolent solutions that will be presented to them by intelligent people like yourself.

Chapter 14 – There is nothing positive about willful ignorance

If you find yourself dissatisfied with the status quo, you may begin to research ways to improve the world. Once you find a few ideas or issues that resonate with you, you might have tried to discuss these feelings with your closest friends and/or family. Chances are, at one time or another you been told things like "stop being so negative," or "can't you just focus on the more positive things in life?"

We can all probably think back on at least one of those frustrating moments where our peers have expected us to share in their blissful ignorance, as they choose to evade reality. Unfortunately, the longer that we ignore the problems that face our species, the worse our predicament becomes. At first glimpse these issues may seem overwhelming and insurmountable but acknowledging the problem is the first step towards freeing your mind and creating a better world for all of us.

In this book we have focused on more positive discussions, but we cannot deny the unpleasant realities of the world that we have to live in. If you had a debilitating illness that could be cured, wouldn't you want to get a diagnosis and immediately start doing what was needed in order to begin healing yourself? Or would you rather do nothing and ignore the disease because it was "negative"? Sadly, we have been led to believe that ignorance is bliss, while it is actually the reason for the majority of the suffering that has taken place throughout history.

If we are not fully aware of the problem, then there is no way that we can possibly improve the quality of life on this Earth. There is simply no excuse for ignoring legitimate problems that need to be fixed, and we certainly should not allow crimes to be committed before our very eyes. Would you allow an attacker to commit murder in front of you without (at the least) calling for help? Would you stand by and wait for someone else to offer their assistance or would you take control of your own life and do what needed to be done?

This is the same situation we find ourselves in. Except the attacker is the institutionalized violence and theft that is the result of Statism. The State does a great job of compartmentalizing the theft and violence so that the average person is unaware that it's even taking place. But once you become aware of injustice, the greatest mistake you can make is to stand by and do nothing.

With the exception of a few radicals every generation, the majority of the human species has remained unwilling, or unable to stand up and challenge the status quo. For centuries, the buck has been passed down the line, and our species has continued to ride this roller coaster of confusion and oppression. In many ways we have come so far and learned so much.

While much of modern civilization still unquestionably accepts slavery, racism, war, and authoritarianism as simple facts of life, many of us are finally beginning to shed some of these neuroses and are starting to consider the fact that a better path may exist. By considering new ideas for governance and law, we can help break ourselves from chains of past dogma. We must now push further into learning, understanding, and teaching these concepts, and then move towards actually building communities that are living examples of these philosophies.

The fact that questioning the status quo is looked at as socially unacceptable allows the population to go on thinking that they are alone in their dissatisfaction. This isolation can lead to feeling weak and powerless. After being discouraged from pursuing change, some people will create justifications for what's going on around them, telling themselves this is the only world that's possible. They may even come to ridicule anyone who challenges their unconsciously created facade. Simply put, the fear of alienation from peers can lead to accepting standards which do not meet our needs or represent our values. Push on, do not be discouraged by people who can not handle reality.

Have compassion and remember that many people are just afraid and are not ready to come to terms with the truth. Like a battered child who cries when being taken away from the "safety" of their abusive parents, you may feel comfort in unacceptable situations simply because you are familiar with them. Much like the child, we need to break free from the familiar confines of our abuse and oppression.

This condition is known as "Stockholm syndrome." Stockholm syndrome is typically used to describe hostages who develop positive feelings for their kidnapper because they are dependent upon them for sustenance. When we apply this concept to the macrocosm of our civilization, we find that people living under a system of authoritarianism exhibit these same characteristics. This concept has been illustrated many times in the past, such as the allegory of the cave from Plato's Republic.

There is nothing positive about running away from freedom and putting off peace. One of the most important steps you can take is to learn as much as you can about how to fix the problems that you see taking place in our world.

Sheltering ourselves from the harshness of our reality will only foster a more toxic and oppressive world for future generations. Embrace the opportunity to create a better vision for tomorrow by changing your thoughts and actions today.

Chapter 15 – Crabs in a bucket

Sometimes it helps to use metaphors to describe the current situations that we are living under to help people see what is right in front of them. The violence and twisted mentality that consumes many cultures around the world is difficult for someone to notice when they have grown up around it, and know nothing else.

Recently, I came across an extremely interesting concept that does a really good job at depicting the current mentality that many people have in their personal relationships as well as their business and political ventures. That is the "crab mentality" which looks at the world as a zero sum game, where there is no such thing as a mutually beneficial exchange. Every situation has winners and losers with this world view, and everyone is out to make someone else a loser. In reality, there are solutions that people can come to without getting hostile with one another, that leads to an outcome where everyone involved is better off than they were before.

Crab mentality is an expression most popular among Filipinos, and was first coined by writer Ninotchka Rosca, in reference to the phrase crabs in a bucket. The phrase describes a way of thinking that is along the same lines of, *"if I can't have it, neither can you."*

The metaphor refers to a pot of crabs, each of which could easily escape from the pot individually, but instead, they grab at each other in a useless "king of the hill" competition which prevents any from escaping and ensures their collective demise. The analogy in human behavior is that members of a group will attempt to "pull down" (negate or diminish the importance of) any member who achieves success beyond the others.

This mentality is probably relevant to almost anyone's life, as we can see it all around us, especially in the social institutions that hold us hostage. Most people look at their everyday encounters as if they were all zero sum games, where they can only get ahead by knocking someone else down. Isn't it possible for everyone to just do their own thing, and use their intellect to work things out when they get in each other's way?

This seems like a far safer and more productive way of doing business than we see today, where many people think that they only way to get ahead is to cut others down. The mainstream culture has yet to catch onto this concept, but that doesn't mean that we have to stagnate with them. In our everyday encounters, business interactions and especially our conflicts, we can take the high road by using our intellect to meet our needs without violating the rights of others. Even in today's world, with seemingly limited resources we can still all get by without slaughtering each other and stirring up trouble.

Tools For Action: NVC, Meditation, and Positive Affirmations

In the first book of *The Conscious Resistance* trilogy we briefly explored the idea of "conscious healing", using various tools and exercises to provoke deep introspection and reflection. We discussed meditation, psychedelics, flotation tanks, yoga, conscious language, and positive affirmations.

Our goal was to inspire the reader to delve deeper into these various modalities and decide what, if any, practices promoted personal and spiritual growth. For this book, we decided to expand upon a few of these practices to provide a better understanding of how to incorporate mindfulness into your daily life. We will be exploring Non-Violent Communication (NVC), meditation, and positive affirmations. If you are interested in these topics, please pursue further research for individual healing.

Chapter 16 - 8 ways to change society without the political process

When a problem occurs or when something is wrong we have traditionally been conditioned to find someone who is "in charge", a final arbiter of decision making who will have all of the answers and know all of the right things to say and do.

Typically, those who have found themselves "in charge" are no more qualified or knowledgeable than those who are not, yet nonetheless these false prophets continue to swindle generation after generation of people.

The worst thing about this whole situation is that these so called "authorities" maintain a monopoly on problem solving, meaning they are really the only ones who are allowed to solve problems. Thus over time people begin to believe that those in authority are the only ones who are actually capable of solving problems, when in reality, they are no more qualified than anyone else.

If we apply this understanding to the realm of government, it is not difficult to see that the current system of electoral politics is not an effective or moral way for people to actually create meaningful change in their communities and the planet as a whole. Year after year, administration after administration the faces change, but the oppression continues to escalate.

Even if your vote is actually counted, which it probably isn't, it still won't matter who wins in the end anyway because they are all going to carry out the exact same policies with just slightly rhetoric behind them. It should be obvious by now that this system is not only inherently corrupt, but is also failing miserably and currently in the process of collapse.

So what do we do? How do we solve these problems? Do we look to authority? Do we put someone else in charge? Of course not! How has that been working out for us all along? Not so well, right?

Yet when I suggest that everyone needs give up on voting and take matters into their own hands in their personal lives, people always seem to get the impression that I am suggesting they "do nothing". In reality the complete opposite is true. I am suggesting that they actually get out and do something to make an impact on the problems that bother them instead of just pushing a button in an election booth, throwing the problem on some politician's lap and thinking that something is actually going to get done.

If anything, that political approach that I just described is the lazy way of going about change, but actually working on solutions yourself is truly meaningful action. There are a ton of ways that you can contribute to helping the global situation without politics. In fact, you will do much better than the politicians at actually achieving the goal. Below are just a few ways that we have recently seen people solving problems in their community by themselves, without the government.

(1) Opt Out in Every Way Possible – Non-Compliance is a long-term strategy and won't achieve overnight results, but this is still a necessary part of this social evolution that I am speaking of. Opting out is a way of pulling your support out of the system, and putting your support in something that will eventually outshine the system and make it obsolete. That is a lot of the idea behind pulling yourself out of the political process and refusing to vote. Voting takes a lot of time and energy, especially if you are donating money to political parties and campaigning for candidates. Opting out will instantly free up that time, energy and money for causes that will be more effective in achieving your goal of improving society.

(2) Be Your Own President – Presidents are not "leaders" as the masquerade to be, they are appointed masters who seek to control the thoughts and actions of large groups of people. You have the choice to disobey any random code or policy that doesn't stand up to the non-aggression principle and natural law.

Exercising that choice is a way of finding freedom in a seemingly unfree world. If you break government laws and no one gets hurt in the process, and no property has been damaged or stolen, then you have done nothing wrong. Be your own master instead of letting someone else control your behavior.

(3) Campaign for Philosophy – After watching puppet after puppet go through office we should all know by now that "getting the right guy in there" isn't any kind of possibility, and even it was a possibility, it would be like giving a really nice guy a sledgehammer to repair a complicated supercomputer.

What really needs to happen is an advancement of philosophy and a change in the way that this species looks at the world. All of the answers for exactly how the future will be built is not yet known and truly unpredictable, but the problems in our current system are obvious enough that they are easy to identify. The fundamental flaws with our traditional way of life as a species is that it has been acceptable for people to force their will on one another, through both private and political means. As a result, violence has plagued our species for ages when we could have easily shed this neurotic tendency just after the stone ages.

For centuries humanity has been trapped in this loop of violence because a philosophical advancement has failed to occur. We have known the path to take for ages, we all talk about it in every culture, in the hypocritical rhetoric of every government.

Equal rights and universal standards, peace, freedom and justice. These are the ideals that we all speak of, but many fail to live by. These are the ideals that will change the world if embraced, but it is not going to happen by voting an aristocratic liar into a position of power. It will only happen through intelligent people talking about these ideas and coming up with new ways to actually integrate them into society.

(4) Support or Start Mutual Aid Groups – As an article pointed out this week, mutual aid groups were one of the most popular ways that people ensured the welfare of their families and neighbors before the government created programs to make everyone depend on them for help.

Years later we can see the results of this approach, as these programs are in total disarray because their purpose was never actually to help people, and those involved have no real incentive to make these programs productive because they aren't even a part of the community that depends on them. This is what makes mutual aid groups different.

First off, these are all programs which are joined by choice and funded voluntarily and they allow people to directly interact with whoever they are helping and with whoever is helping them. These programs are highly efficient and realistic even in today's world. A variation of this idea is already becoming popular among jobless people in Spain and other areas of Europe, where citizens have been using mutual aid organizations called time banks, to help each other weather the tough times.

(5) Support or Create Alternative Currency – There are alternative currencies popping up all over the world, and all over the Internet as well. Bitcoin has been the primary currency used online, but the market is open to competitors so Bitcoin will have to actually continue to satisfy customers, or it will surely give way to a more user friendly currency, something that the Federal Reserve System has never had to do because they monopolize the currency.

For close communities and urban markets coupon based, community backed currencies are starting to develop, which allow people to opt out of the Federal Reserve System, and barter with their neighbors using a mutually agreed upon medium of exchange which has no tie to politics at all. In Baltimore many use "Bnotes" to trade amongst themselves, out west they have something called mountain hours that works in much the same way.

If there is one of these currencies in your community see what you can do to get involved, if not there are plenty of places online that will tell you how to start this kind of project yourself.

(6) Support or Create a Community or Personal Garden – Food prices are getting high and quality is

63

getting lower, making times extremely tough for anyone trying to be healthy. If there is already a garden in your community, try to get involved and support them as much as possible. If there isn't one in your community, think about starting one yourself!

(7) Support or Create Alternative Media – It's no secret that the mainstream media is a dying entity that has totally lost the confidence of the general population. CNN has been reporting an 80% decrease year after year, and the outlets on either side of the aisle aren't doing much better either.

They are all losing their audience to the people-powered alternative media which is run by large networks of individual activists, most of which really need and deserve some support from the people who appreciate their media. Cancelling your cable subscription and putting that money towards your favorite alternative media organization is a big step in shifting the control of information back into the hands of free people exchanging ideas, instead of government monopolists.

(8) Act with Kindness and Compassion in Your Own Life – Self-explanatory, be excellent to each other.

Chapter 17 - What is Meditation and how do I meditate?

As we outline in *Reflections on Anarchy and Spirituality,* meditation is a beneficial practice as old as human life. As long as human beings have been conscious, we have come to nature for quiet contemplation and reflection. So what exactly is meditation?

The dictionary definition of meditation is, *"an act or practice that brings you to a place of contemplation, a state of relaxation."*

The consistent application of bringing one's attention to the present moment is key to any form of meditation. This means that nearly any experience can be meditative. A bike ride, a walk under the stars, writing poetry, or any practice that offers individual quiet time within your own heart and mind can be considered a form of meditation.

Over time, various teachers organized their specific meditation practices into cohesive styles and philosophies, each with its own instructions and insights. Around the 5th and 6th centuries BCE, Confucian and Taoist meditations appear in China, and Hindu, Jain, and Buddhist meditations developed in India.

These various schools of meditation taught different methods for remaining in the present moment, some involving the counting of breaths, contemplative thought, or repeating sacred words and sounds known as Mantras.

There are also different types of meditation positions. Some schools practice sitting cross-legged ("lotus" or "half lotus"), walking, or lying down meditation. You also may have noticed that certain traditions will feature symbolic hand gestures and positions during their meditation. These are known as mudras and are found in Hindu and Buddhist practices. People also meditate for different reasons. Most people would say that meditation can be a religious or spiritual experience, while others find it to be a helpful relaxation and anger management tool.

For example, if you are dealing with stress and looking for answers, you may choose to focus on finding the source of your stress, or attempt to clear your mind of all distractions. Different situations require different solutions.

For those interested in learning different types of meditations, we recommend Transcendental Meditation, Zen Buddhism, Mindfulness Meditation, and Contemplative Prayer. We would like to offer a couple methods that we have found to be helpful for general meditation.

First, think of a time that you can meditate on a daily, or weekly basis. The more consistent you are with meditation, the more mindful you will become in your everyday life. Once you have worked out your schedule, decide if you would like to focus on sitting meditation or lying down. Finally, for those who say they cannot meditate, we say, be patient!

You cannot expect to go from bombarding yourself with stimuli and distractions to a perfectly still mind overnight. Keep at it and you can push past the static. Try the following four exercises to get you started.

Clearing The Mind

If your goal is to clear your mind, begin by sitting cross-legged with a straight, firm back. Position your shoulders above your hips and place your hands open on top of your knees. You can keep your eyes open and stare softly about four or five feet in front of you, or close your eyes.

Take slow, deep breaths. Focus on your breaths. As you breathe deep in through your nose count "one". Exhale and repeat to yourself "one". Continue this process as long as you can. You will find yourself lost in thought within a couple of numbers. This is perfectly normal and not a reason to be discouraged. Your mind wants to think, to fill the quiet, dull spaces with chatter. When you realize that you stopped counting after 3 and began thinking about your next blog post, take a deep breath and start over.

Think of these thoughts like passing clouds, acknowledge them, give thanks for them, and then return your attention to counting. In a 5-minute session you might not make it past 5, but that's not the goal. You are not attempting to suffocate or ignore your thoughts, but simply focusing on being present. The goal is to simply "be" in that moment, without stress or concern. However, if a situation or person continues to appear in your meditations it may be a sign that you need to focus and work to find clarity.

Finding Clarity

For this meditation, you can set up exactly the same as you are when clearing your mind. The difference here, is that instead of clearing the mind, you will relax and focus on a specific situation or person that needs your attention. This could be a relationship that you are uncertain of, or a friend that you want to celebrate.

Whether for clarity or to affirm the positive, you want to sit and take a deep breath as you focus. If you are looking for answers, take the time to imagine the ideal outcome and consider the situation from the perspective of everyone involved.

If you are giving thanks for a new opportunity or friendship, focus your mind on expressing gratitude and appreciation. Taking time for reflection during uncertain times helps one develop a predisposition for mindfulness over impulsiveness.

Connecting to the Earth

This exercise can be done lying down or sitting. Either way, you want to begin with slow, deep breaths. Imagine that you are connected to the Earth physically and energetically.

All the power of the planet is flowing up from the ground in the form of a white light. Imagine this white light coming up from the Earth into the base of your body. The light runs up through your feet, into your waist, connecting to your heart, and out through the crown of your head.

As the light flows through each piece of your body, imagine you are being cleansed. You feel this white light removing the stresses from each piece of you. As the light flows out the top of your head, it goes up into the sky and back down into the Earth to start all over again. Continue imagining and feeling this light for at least 15 minutes.

Thanking your body

This meditation is meant to be done lying down with your arms at your side. Beginning with your toes, you are going to slowly move and become aware of each piece of your body. Imagine that your awareness is within your toes, and gives thanks to them.

Think of all the work your toes and feet do to make sure you can live your life. Take your time slowly going from your toes, to your feet, to your ankles, your shins, etc. and give thanks to each individual piece of your body. Recognize the power of each piece of you.

Chapter 18 - Non-Violent Communication

Language is, without a doubt, one of the most important and profound developments in human history. It has allowed us to describe the world we live in and express ourselves to one another. Language lays the foundation for our belief systems and also our idiosyncrasies. Our view of the universe is also shaped by the words that we use to describe what we see and experience. Written language is especially important because it immortalizes information and makes it possible for humans to record an extremely detailed history.

In order to surpass the systemic violence we see in much of our world, we must expand the limits of our vocabulary. Anyone can contribute to the positive expansion of their culture's vocabulary, and tear down the linguistic barriers set by those who keep us mentally enslaved. Advancing our communication skills is an essential step towards achieving world peace.

One man who has worked tirelessly on communication is traveler and psychologist Marshall Rosenberg. Rosenberg is responsible for developing a new way of speaking which he calls Non Violent Communication (NVC) or Compassionate Communication. This method of communication is simple and has had profound success all over the world, from the feuding tribes of the southern hemisphere to the broken homes of modern America. Marshall recognized that all human language is filled with traps that inevitably lead to conflict, these traps are trigger words which he referred to as "jackal language".

Jackal language consists of words that imply guilt, humiliation, shame, blame, coercion, or threats. Marshall believes that this kind of language and interaction is not a natural process, but a byproduct of the "culture of domination" that he believes has consumed our species for at least eight thousand years. We agree with his assertion. To resolve conflicts, it is necessary for us to avoid using jackal language, and learn to be empathetic when working out our problems.

According to NVC, conflict arises between two or more people when someone in the equation has needs which aren't being met. This is the root cause for humans acting out and the reason why some people are oftentimes unhappy with the actions of others. In most conflicts, these issues are never addressed. Instead of identifying everyone's feelings and needs in order to work towards a solution, the two parties begin a battle of blaming, which neither side can ever truly win.

Nonviolent communication is a very easy method to explain, but can be difficult to master. One of the most difficult parts of the process to actually grasp is the very first step - observation. In times of conflict, many of us are very quick to confuse judgments with observations.

An observation would be *"our project is due next week"*. In this case you are only stating the facts of the situation, you are not making any judgments. A judgment relating to this observation would be *"our project is due next week and you haven't done a damn thing, I have done all of the work, you are lazy"*.

This is an example of the kind of judgments that cause a lot of arguments and miscommunication. It is very common for conflicts to be filled with judgments and labels that only push the conversation into a more negative direction. Don't get discouraged with yourself if you find it difficult to speak without passing judgments or using jackal language, as these are both things that are fundamentally woven into our language and seem natural to most people.

Once an observation is made, it's time for the parties involved to express their feelings on the subject to establish a mutual understanding. For example, one could say, *"our project is due next week, and I'm very worried about our grade, what can we do to make sure we pass?"*

In situations of conflict, it is an unmet need that is causing discontent, so the objective of the conversation is to identify the needs which are causing the feelings. Once everyone's needs are on the table it becomes very easy to see a possible solution in which everyone's needs are met and the conflict can be resolved.

This was a very quick and basic introduction to nonviolent communication but there are many books written by Marshall Rosenberg that discuss his theories in greater detail.

There are also local NVC groups around the world where you can learn the techniques. Marshall Rosenberg is just one great mind in a sea of millions, and it is very possible for his method to be someday improved upon, or for an entirely different communication method to develop. In fact, it is probably necessary for each generation to constantly be working to improve our language, so it can be a tool of expression, rather than a tool of oppression.

Chapter 19 - Affirming the Positive and Manifesting Reality

In our first book, we discussed the connection between Creative Visualization, Positive Affirmation, and Manifestation. When you exercise our imagination and visualize that which you hope to create or achieve, you attach a powerful symbol to your vision.

By creating "vision boards" with words and images that represent our desired goals, or by simply meditating on what we would like to see in our lives, we remind ourselves of the steps we must take to achieve those goals. By sitting in quiet reflection and allowing our minds to clear of distraction, we can achieve all we desire.

Through visualization, we can see, smell, taste, hear, and touch the ideal situation we are trying to manifest, and work through the difficult problems we may be facing. Once you are comfortable with visualizing your path, it is important to affirm the path. This is where positive affirmation comes into play.

Positive affirmation is a highly effective method of programming oneself. We face external programming every day through the corporate media, the government, and those we communicate with. One way or another, whether by our own doing or some external force, we will be programmed.

The mind is much like a computer that can be loaded with a variety of programs. Many of us buy into cultural and environmental programming that does not empower us as individuals, but rather teaches us to doubt our potential and capabilities. We must take steps to deprogram ourselves from such destructive thinking. With daily affirmations, we can create a positive, compassionate view of ourselves and of the world around us. By using affirming statements, such as "I AM...", we allow our minds to let go of negative habits and begin to rewrite the pathways our thoughts take.

For example – perhaps your insecurities are a constant prison, a paralysis that limits your social life as much as your internal world. By changing your internal self-talk that says you are incapable of certain tasks or that other humans view you in a negative light, and affirming, "I am capable, I am deserving of love and compassion," you can overcome a lifetime of unnecessary insecurities and doubts.

Over time this reprogramming of your mind becomes habit. Rather than buying into the limiting thoughts when they appear, you are able to say, "No, Thank you, I no longer need you!" and instead tell yourself, "I am capable, I am loved, I am becoming stronger every day in every way."

This simple act can have long-lasting, life-changing effects. Through creative visualization and daily affirmations, we are not only changing our state of mind and the way we look at our world, but we are energetically altering the course of our lives.

Manifestation is the power of watching an idea go from a seed in your mind, to a daily focus, to a physical reality. Manifestation is the culmination of an empowered individual understanding what they want, making a conscious choice to pursue that goal, calling out to the universe for assistance, and taking steps in the physical world to bring that idea into reality.

These tools are not simply a method of praying or wishing away the problems we face. We must remember that the power of the mind is assisted by actions taken by the physical body. Through personal responsibility, determination, and a focused work ethic we can produce the results we seek and have everything we desire.

We would like to offer the following six affirmations to help you get started. Our experience has shown that repeating these aloud in the morning (before you get distracted by work, school, etc.) is a great way to start the day with mindfulness. Before you start, find a quiet place to relax. You can do this in front of a mirror, or sitting down meditating while you repeat the affirmations. Once you have found your spot, take a deep breath, fill up your lungs with as much air as possible, and then slowly release your breath through your nostrils. Do this a few times until you are completely relaxed and then begin your affirmations. Feel free to adjust the words and themes to suit your specific situation. Wherever and whenever you decide to do your affirmations, remember to be consistent. Doing these on a daily basis, as often as needed, will promote gratitude and empowerment.

Choosing Self-Control

This one is beneficial for when you are having a rough day. It will help to remind you to be thankful. When you find yourself getting agitated, or angry, slow down and repeat these words:

Today I give thanks to the Great Spirit that flows in all life. I am filled with gratitude for another day, another set of moments that allow me to create the world of my own choosing.

I am indebted to my friends and family for being constant reflections of the lessons that I need to see.

Today, in this moment, I am getting stronger in every way. My ability to take on difficult situations and to see the lessons is constantly growing.
I no longer need self-pity, grudges, or anger.
I choose to see all that comes my way as motivation for my future endeavors.

I am powerful. I am free.
I am powerful. I am free.
I am the only person who can dictate my emotions and actions.
I choose to let my thoughts, my words, and actions from this moment on flow from a place of love.
I choose to let my thoughts, my words, and actions from this moment on flow from a place of love.

Choosing Self Forgiveness

It's important for us to remember to forgive and love ourselves. The sooner we heal and love ourselves, the sooner we can amplify and emanate that energy out into the world.

Today, in this moment, I am filled with gratitude for my path and the lessons presented to me.
I choose to see any and all hardships as temporary, and as opportunities for growth.

I forgive myself for my past mistakes and flaws.
With each passing moment I am becoming better, stronger, and more compassionate.

I understand that life is a constant learning experience.
I see any bumps in the road as possibilities for alternative outcomes.

I remain committed to my path as a beautiful, free, independent human being.
I choose to remain open to the lessons that manifest on my path.
I remember that I am the master of my own life and the creator of my destiny.

Today I choose (what do you want to manifest today?).

Being Present

Today I give thanks for the present moment, the endless, repeatless NOW.
I give thanks for endless "NOW's" to manifest my highest good.

I am completely present in this time and space.
I choose to "be here now" in whatever I am doing.

In this moment I choose to be the best secretary, the best artist, the best musician, the best chef, the best mechanic, the best husband, wife, and the best human I can be.

I choose to let the distractions of my active mind float past my awareness like passing clouds.
I choose to embrace my present circumstances and to "be the Buddha" in this moment.

Letting Go

Today, in this moment, I choose to reflect on any and all situations that might not be contributing to my highest good.

I choose to examine the conflict, external and internal, and decide whether I can rectify the situation.
I choose to come from a place of love and compassion, and make a decision that will be best for all involved.

If, upon examining the situation, I find no solution, I choose to let go.
I choose to see the positive, the lessons gained from the experience and let go for my health and sanity.
I give thanks for these experiences and the lessons they have provided.

I choose to be in control of my life and my experiences. I choose to remain open to new lessons and open to letting go when necessary.

Finding Balance

Today, in this moment, I am thankful for my strength and my success.
I am grateful for the perceived failures that are lessons for me on my path.
In this moment, I choose balance.
I choose to release that which is weighing me down or keeping me in the clouds.
I strive for an acceptance of all my emotions, good, bad, and everything in between.
I accept and own all my emotions.

I choose to listen to my body, mind and spirit, and move in a direction that stabilizes me and promotes balance.
I choose to remember that balance must start with my thoughts, move to my words and then my actions. Only then will the balance be long lasting and genuine.
I recognize that this is a continuous process and allow myself to stumble so I may pick myself up stronger than ever.

Celebrating YOU!

In this moment I choose to accept my greatness, my
potential, and my innate power.
I choose to recognize this greatness, potential and power in
all living beings I see.

I am letting go of all thoughts that work to limit my
greatness, potential and power.
I am opening my heart to experiences that celebrate my full
potential.

Celebrating The Sun

This is a simple thank you to the Sun. Try creating your own affirmations that give thanks to the elements that sustain all life.

Today, in this moment, I am thankful for the boundless, amazing, magnificent beauty that is the Sun.
I am thankful for the constant light, for the source of heat, for the source of food, for the source of energy that provides endlessly.

I am thankful for myself, to my own light.
I am thankful for opportunities to recognize how bright I truly shine.

In this moment I release all doubt, all fear, all elements that are not currently serving my highest light, my highest good.

In this moment I choose to resonate with truth, compassion, justice, freedom, and to be a shining light in my universe for others that surround me.

Our Journeys: About the Authors:

John Vibes

Since as far back as I can remember I largely rejected the cultural traditions that I was born into, because they seemed unnatural, irrational and oppressive. School was difficult because even from a young age I refused to conform and somehow understood that I wasn't going to learn anything of value in school.

Most of my teachers in elementary school resented me because I would bring in books on topics that I was interested in and I would read them to myself while the class was going over their indoctrinating lesson. By the time high school came around I was so sick of the whole thing that I spent my class time sleeping, drinking and doing drugs, and from time to time I would still read. The oppressive nature of the school system only pushed me to hold greater resentment against authority and mainstream society. Unfortunately, that resentment pushed me toward some naive conclusions.

Although I had my suspicions about society and the status quo, I was still heavily conditioned by media and operating on a fairly low level of consciousness. I was still seeing the world in black and white terms and was pushed towards ideas like Satanism and Communism, because I was so turned off with the typical mainstream culture that I was subject to, that I just ran in the total opposite direction for solutions. Like many of the pitfalls I encountered, this was a necessary adventure along my path, and vital to my learning experience. Those interests led me to a wide variety of philosophical studies, but nothing would really make sense to me until many years later when I had enough information to get a clear picture of how things really worked. Most of my adolescence was filled with misplaced angst and overindulgence, which I hear is fairly typical. Regular drug tests pushed me towards heavy alcohol and pharmaceutical use, so although I was using psychedelics and researching philosophy I was still very clouded because of the mind numbing chemicals that I was putting into my body and the media that I surrounded myself with.

Through those years I was faced with many synchronistic situations that slowly led me toward a more conscious lifestyle and informed perspective, but it would be many years before I broke free from the state of sleep that I was in.

There is no doubt that every single one of us has our whole perception of reality crafted by our environment and the things we experience, I'm obviously no different. Like most of the people on the planet I was born into a life of serfdom and grew up being constantly reminded about the struggles and obstacles that came along with financial slavery. Many times I was shown firsthand the senseless violence of war and the threatening oppression of the legal system, as you can tell my story is not unique, almost anyone can relate. The issues that have impacted my life and the ones I discuss in this book affect everyone, they are not limited to my experience.

Things did begin to get a little bit out of the ordinary when I started working at a funeral home at the age of 17. Looking back, it's hard to imagine that I was drawn to that kind of profession, but at the time I was a very confused person. I ended up spending about 6 years as an apprentice mortician and those were quite possibly the most turbulent times of my life. I'm sure that the late teen to young adult phase is no cakewalk for anyone, but my job and my drinking problem seemed to at least keep things interesting.

They say you should never regret anything, and for the most part I agree, but if I could take back anything I wouldn't have let my drinking get so out of hand. At the time I was very ignorant, and underestimated the toxicity of alcohol due to its cultural acceptance. I was left with health problems that I'm still trying to sort out today. I was never an aggressive drunk, but that doesn't mean that I wasn't an extremely stupid drunk that caused a lot of trouble for myself and other people.

Believe it or not it would take an enlightening shamanic experience to make me realize that I was destroying my body and that I should probably phase out my alcohol use. After 7 years of drinking hard liquor on a daily basis it was a lot easier to quit then I ever thought it would be, and with every day that passed I became more conscious of what was going on around me.

Due to my own personal experience and my earlier research into philosophy I was always untrusting of power, government, war, finance, religion and authority in general, but I didn't have enough of the specific background information to fully understand the true nature of our reality. I had a very limited knowledge of occult history for most of my life and was heavily sedated by chemicals and cultural assumptions that I greatly underestimated due to my ignorance.

That all began to change when my physical and mental health started to deteriorate from alcohol abuse, heavy smoking and extremely poor eating habits. I was partying constantly because I was so disgusted with society and the life that seemed to lie before me, because it just seemed so confusing and backwards. I saw a world consumed with greed, violence, pain and misunderstanding for no apparent reason. This wasn't the kind of world I wanted to live in. I didn't want anyone to be subject to violence and I didn't approve of the status quo, but I was so convinced that this was the only world that was possible that I made no attempt to do anything about it and led a hedonistic lifestyle in order to fill a void in my soul.

During that period I was immersed in the heavy metal circuit in Baltimore and although mostly everyone was distracted by sex, drugs n rock n roll, I synchronistically met some activists and artists who were using the scene as a social platform. My new friends and acquaintances taught me all sorts of new information about the monetary system, social engineering and specifically the new world order.

After putting a few tidbits together with the research I had done in the past, light bulbs went off all over the place in my head and I began to scour the internet for more information. There I found piles of documented evidence that supported what I knew all along but had no clue how to put into words. Eventually after enough research, it became easier to find the words and I could accurately explain to myself and others why I disapproved of the status quo and exactly who was responsible for perpetuating it.

Unfortunately, even with my newfound knowledge I was still making poor decisions and still had a very negative outlook. My whole worldview was still heavily conditioned by years of media, schooling, and cultural norms. I was still looking at things in a very nihilistic way, where I had no understanding of the higher spiritual levels that existed or the unbelievable things that could be achieved through love and human cooperation. I really hate to be cliché here, but I was to learn all of this at my first hippy festival. I'm going to spare the names, dates and places out of respect for the promoters, but ill share the basics of what happened. This event was something that I had never experienced before and I had no clue what to expect. It ended up being a whole weekend almost completely removed from the mainstream American culture which had held me prisoner for most of my life.

My many adventures and realizations over that weekend would have a huge impact on my future path and encouraged me to delve deeper into the counter culture. After the enlightening weekend I had at that event. I spent the rest of the summer touring similar festivals on the east coast, seeking to clock more time outside of the mainstream culture and return once again down the rabbit hole.

That summer my travels brought me to an outdoor rave that was on the water. That was probably one of the best parties I had ever been to, until around 3am when fire trucks, cop cars and other emergency vehicles began to surround the event. Things became very frantic at that point and I decided that I should leave the area where everyone had assembled and find another way out.

Just before the area was raided I saw a fishing boat and began to shout to them for help and they came ashore to see what was going on. I offered them 20 dollars to take me and my friends out of harm's way toward where we had parked our car, and luckily the agreed to help us.

That certainly wasn't my first close call with the Gestapo that summer. After a few of these encounters I came to realize that the counter culture truly was outlawed in this Orwellian society I had come to find myself in. I always had a deep suspicion of authority, but now that I had the proper information and witnessed this peaceful culture being demonized by those authoritarian forces, I understood the reality of how our "civilization" operates.

In addition to the personal realizations that came to me at that show I had also made connections which would eventually help me establish myself as a rave promoter. At one of these events I met a promoter from Philly who said he hosted parties at a place called "Gods Basement" and that I should check it out sometime. If it wasn't for that synchronistic random encounter it is highly possible that I never would have wrote this book, thrown a single rave or even met my wife.

Without Gods Basement and the time I spent there I can't even begin to imagine what my life would be like today. While I had been to some club and underground events in the past, Gods Basement was my official introduction into the underground rave scene.

When I started partying at Gods Basement, I was still in that part of my life where I was drinking on a daily basis and working at a funeral home in Baltimore. Nearly every day after work I would stop at local bars to kill time before traffic died down and most times I ended up at a place called The Black Hole. Eventually I took on a second job there working the door during rock and hip hop shows to make some extra money.

Eventually, The Black Hole began getting involved in raves after a friend of mine made a suggestion to the owner. I helped book and promote a few shows there when things were starting up but was always helping other crews, doing my own shows never really crossed my mind at that point. After a while I began to spend most of my time in Philly and New York networking and promoting for shows at Gods Basement and the The Black Hole, with my wife Kali. At the time we had just recently met, but now we are happily married and I don't know what I would do without her.

Gods Basement was one of the main party spots on the east coast when I began promoting, and The Black Hole was still getting itself established and building its base crowd. Gods Basement is still to this day one of the most awesome venues I have ever been to, and I feel extremely lucky for the time I was able to spend there. As they say though, all good things must come to an end.

When Gods Basement came under fire I learned just how corrupt and one sided the media is first hand. At the time I was familiar with media bias but I was still under the impression that the talking heads on the news were just mistaken with good intentions. However, as I would learn, the media consistently and deliberately constructs lies, falsifies reports and intentionally spins stories in order to uphold the status quo.

I'll be the first one to admit that wild things happen at raves, but they still offer a much safer and more peaceful environment than the average rock or hip hop concert that is advertised on mainstream television and radio. Gods Basement was eventually closed after an ignorant and close minded mother who didn't want her 18 year old child going to the events, reported the underground venue to the local news. Instead of playing an active role in her child's life and attempting to understand what was going on in her child's mind, this parent decided to force her will onto an entire culture. With her face and voice disguised, she appeared on the news calling for the shutdown of Gods Basement.

This bigoted testimony was presented with fake video footage of kids doing various drugs, but long time patrons of Gods Basement could see that the clips which showed this were not even filmed at that venue. After the initial story ran, the NBC news channel received so much feedback defending rave culture that they were forced to run a second story to apparently show the other side of the argument.

As expected, that second segment was a total whitewash, where all legitimate complaints about the hit piece from the day before were mocked and marginalized, leaving the viewer with a skewed version of events. The fact that the promotion crews involved with the venue ran regular charity events and gave back to the community was completely left out of the reports and when it was time for the crew to make a statement their words were distorted and put in a context that made us look careless and unintelligent.

The lies and attacks from the media eventually did result in the downfall of Gods Basement. When things got too crazy in Philly, I returned to Baltimore with a new direction and new connections that I developed working as a street promoter for Tru Skool Productions, the crew that ran Gods Basement.

By spring of 2008 I began to start thinking about doing my own shows because there were some elements that I had witnessed in the parties up north, which were lacking from the events in Baltimore and DC. The shows up north had a more underground feel, with themes, hard dance music and decorations, whereas the parties in my area were club events, not raves.

So I approached the The Black Hole with my plan and by June of that year I began hosting my own underground themed events under Good Vibes Promotions. The name was just something that came naturally to me, almost at the same time that I had decided to start a crew.

From the first show on things were great, the parties were awesome, crowds came out of nowhere and packed the place every month, things were looking very promising. The only problem we really had was that the venue was in a residential area and we got harassed by the cops on a pretty regular basis.

The place never backed down though and launched their own lawsuits on the police department armed with video evidence and countless eyewitnesses on their side, including myself. Unfortunately, years later the police launched a full scale raid and shut down the business, bringing an era to an end and putting many nonviolent human beings in cages. This situation was of course one of the many times in which I experienced the corruption of the legal system first hand.

In the beginning, I knew I enjoyed themed events but I was having a lot of trouble coming up with themes on my own. The names for the first few events that I hosted actually came from friends, for some reason my creativity seemed to be blocked.

This was around the same time where I had really been getting deep in my activist research, spending up to 6 hours a day or more studying the things I have discussed in this book. It must have been very obvious to everyone around me that occult history and activism had pretty much consumed my interest, because many of my friends suggested that I themed my events around the things I was researching. The idea was brilliant and suddenly I no longer had any problem coming up with creative ideas for my shows. I did parties about sacred geometry, the Wall Street bailouts, free "end the fed" shows on tax day and many other events aimed at subtly educating the people who came out.

Eventually I was able to get a website set up thanks to the generosity of the raver who set up the domain and taught me the basics of the software. The website allowed me to host hundreds of educational activist documentaries and post independent news in an organized format on a daily basis. The website really took my research to a new level and eventually resulted in the book that you have just read.

I'm not the best writer in the world, I'm certainly not the best rave promoter and I'm not any smarter than your average person either. I have just spent my life confused about the social structure and why people behave the way they do, so I have continued to seek answers with every passing day. As time passed and I began to piece together more information I realized that most of what I was taught throughout my whole life was untrue. I had always suspected this but since I didn't have all of the information, I wasn't able to fully understand or specifically describe what I knew in my soul.

I have always had a mentality that was in line with the principals of non-aggression and I was always aware that the major establishments in society didn't live up to those standards. For most of my life that vague idea was more or less the extent to my understanding of geo political and financial events. That all changed when I started researching things more thoroughly and came across the ideas and pieces of information that are contained in these pages.

Many synchronicities that I experienced during my adventures in the counter culture are eventually what led me to begin writing this book. I never had many resources or big time connections so when I began to think of new ways that I could contribute to the freedom movement, writing seemed like the only real option financially and logistically. Faster computers for video editing, music production software or podcasting equipment were not a financial possibility for me, but luckily writing doesn't cost anything. I knew that my path would be some form of art, because as I expressed many times I feel that human creativity is the only way to put an end to the violence and lack of compassion that is so prevalent in today's culture.

After I released my first book in 2011, I began writing articles for various alternative media sources. After about a year it became apparent that I had chosen a con artist as a publisher, causing me to become very discouraged with that path, so I began getting more involved in public activism. By 2012 I became a daily writer for some of the world's leading alternative media sources. Around that same time, I took on a role as the executive producer of the Bob Tuskin radio show. In 2013, I began taking on more public speaking appearances. Prior to that I had only held seminars at the annual Big Dub Candy Mountain Festival, an outdoor rave event filled with many people that I would consider family. My first two speaking appearances in academic settings came in 2013, with appearances at the Free Your Mind Conference in Philadelphia and the Porcupine Freedom Festival in New Hampshire.

I also acted as a volunteer for all of these events, and eventually became one of the lead organizers for the Free Your Mind Conference. In 2014, Alchemy of the Timeless Renaissance, the book I had worked on for many years, is finally being released in an authorized form. Now I am working on writing more books, putting together events like the raves that I host with Good Vibes Promotions, and also organizing academic events like the Free Your Mind Conference.

John Vibes

Our Journeys: About the Authors:

Derrick Broze

In my short 30 years on this planet I have been a child, a musician, a convict, a promoter, a liar, an activist, a gardener, a spiritual being, journalist and so much more. The last few years of my life I have made major efforts to heal and merge all these aspects of myself into one balanced human. It is not always an easy task but I believe this book will be an important part of that effort.

Since 2011 I have been pulled further into the direction of self-exploration and activism. Most of my experience with activism, and specifically Anarchy, has been through underground book stores, and infoshops. These community centers embodied the spirit of mutual aid and breaking down false barriers.

Over time I learned that my politics did not agree with many of those who were a part of this culture but I always loved the communal, non-oppressive environment. This experience helped shaped my views and understanding of Left Anarchist politics. Without those lessons I do not think I would have come to understand Anarchy as I do now.

While I was examining my physical world and working to better understand the nature of government, I was also beginning to better know my internal world. Since I have already mentioned my time behind bars and traveling on the road I will leave those details out. Needless to say those experiences shaped my outlook greatly. Without these experiences I do not believe I would have been able to get at the root causes of my pain and begin the ever-important process of healing.

It was also my time as a provider of LSD that I first began to question the nature of reality and to push the boundaries of my belief systems. Later I would discover meditation which would set the stage for my spiritual pursuits.

By 2012 I had decided that I could no longer work for "The Man" and would rather be poor (or even homeless) if it meant I could be happy and free. Thankfully my activism began to get noticed in Houston and around the globe and in the Spring of 2013 John Vibes helped me get my first writing job. Since that time my work and network has increased and as of the printing of this book I am writing for 4 different publications, in addition to my still ongoing community activism in Houston.

My path towards Panarchy and Spiritual Awareness was equally shaped by my time as a promoter of music and art events. In 2009 I started a booking collective called Visionary Noise. Since that time I have worked with a partner to turn VN into one of the most recognized names in promotion in the Houston area.

Through promoting events and local shows, I have come to understand that any sustainable movement aiming to create change must be rooted in the community. We cannot just promote ideas related to economics and philosophy but we must strive to engage the artist communities to help foster a new culture that reflects our values.

Equally important has been my time as a gardener. My 2011 bike tour gave me an opportunity to spend time on farms to witness firsthand the power and beauty of a self-sufficient lifestyle. Upon returning from my bike tour I started my own gardening business, Organic Gardens For All, and have worked to bring the people of Houston closer to the ideas of home and community gardens. I have learned so much through my time in the soil and Sun.

Now here I am in 2015: a journalist; an activist; a gardener; a spiritual student; musician; promoter; and who knows what else is next! In the immediate future I plan to promote the ideas contained within these pages as well as move further into living the Agorist principles and lifestyle.

Thank you for reading our book! See you out there in the Free World!

Derrick Broze

Acknowledgements - Derrick Broze

This book would not have been possible without the many amazing, supportive people I have been blessed to meet on my path. There are far too many to name them all so I apologize ahead of time if you do not see your name here.

First off, Thank You to the creator force that shapes all paths and experiences. Thank you to my family for always being supportive. Thank you to Be Amor for many lessons. I appreciate you for walking with me on this journey.

A special thanks to Micah Jackson for valuable insight and education on philosophy.

A big thanks to The Conscious Resistance Network team: Damon Shaw, Danilo Cuellar, Katy DeFazio, Francis Ysdoras, Brandon BC, Tryp, Jeffer Thomasson, Anthony Aguero, Sam Wagner, Michael King, Joe Martino of Collective-Evolution.com, and of course Neil Radimaker.

And in no particular order thank you to the following people for inspiration and strength: Adam Kokesh, Ben Swann, John Bush, Catherine Bleish, Huang Po, Samuel E. Konkin III, Ernesto Jara, Jade The Creator, Oskar Yetzirah, Joe Medina, Paul Osman, Cody Adams, Colin Staffieri, my brothers in MANINKARI, Dillon Loftus, Edgar Amador, Britney Miranda, Jacquelyn Samperi, Richard Dee, Joe Zenner, Randa Fox, Hailey Spates, Alex Fischer, and Rosie Soto. Thank you to all the Houston Free Thinkers and my spiritual family for holding it down in H-Town.

Acknowledgements - John Vibes

This list will be short because I have had so many great people help me along my path that I don't want to risk leaving any of them out.

However, I would like to give a special thanks to the sites that I currently write for, thefreethoughtproject.com, trueactivst.com, theantimedia.org, punkrocklibertarians.com, notbeinggoverned.com, as well as the sites that gave me my start, activistpost.com and intellihub.com.

I would also like to thank Mark Passio for his confidence in entrusting me with the Free Your Mind Conference and Bob Tuskin for giving me my first radio interview.

None of this would be accomplished if it was not for my wife and family, so I am eternally grateful for their support and guidance.

And lastly, thank you to my brother Derrick Broze for joining me on this important piece of work and all of the financial contributors who made this project a reality.

Edited By: Edited by Darcey Kobs and Shane Radiff

Cover Art: Justin Eyecue M3 Designs

Peace.Love.Anarchy

To find out more about The Conscious Resistance and Brain Paper Publishing, or to order more books please visit the following websites.

www.theconsciousresistance.com

www.brainpaperpublishing.com

Made in the USA
San Bernardino, CA
10 July 2018